CHILDREN'S FAVOURITE
BIBLE STORIES

The Life of Jesus

Based on stories by Patricia Hunt

Illustrated by Angus McBride

Ward Lock Limited · London

Text © Patricia Hunt 1981, 1984
Illustrations © Ward Lock Limited 1981

This edition first published in Great Britain in 1984
by Ward Lock Limited, 82 Gower Street,
London WC1E 6EQ, a Pentos Company.

Filmset in Bookman by Text Filmsetters Ltd,
Orpington, Kent

Printed and bound in Italy by
Poligrafici Calderara, Bologna

British Library Cataloguing in Publication Data

Hunt, Patricia
   The life of Jesus – (Children's favourite Bible
   stories; 1)
   1. Jesus Christ – Biography – Juvenile literature
   1. Title   II. McBride, Angus   III. Series
   232.9′01   BT302

   ISBN 0-7063-6321-3

Contents

The Birth of Jesus

In the little town of Nazareth in Galilee there lived a good and gentle young woman named Mary who was engaged to a local carpenter named Joseph, a fine, kindly man.

One day Mary had a surprising visitor. An angel named Gabriel suddenly appeared before her. 'Hail, Mary,' He said, 'the Lord is with you.'

Mary was puzzled, for she did not understand what the angel's visit could mean.

'Do not be afraid, Mary,' said the angel, 'for you are to have a son, and His name will be Jesus. He will be the son of the Most High God, and He will be a king whose kingdom will never end.'

'How can this be?' asked Mary, greatly worried, 'I have no husband.'

'The Holy Spirit will come to you,' answered the angel, 'so that God's power will be with you, for the child will be the Son of God.'

'I am God's servant,' said Mary quietly. 'May it happen as you have said.'

And then the angel left her.

Bethlehem

Now Palestine in those days was part of the Roman Empire, and some time

after the appearance of the angel to Mary and Joseph, the Roman Emperor, Caesar Augustus, issued an order. He commanded that everyone should be 'enrolled'. To do this, each person was to return to his home town or city to register himself.

For Joseph this meant a long and tiring journey from Nazareth in Galilee southwards to Bethlehem in Judea. Joseph had to make careful preparations, especially as Mary was going with him and would soon be having her baby.

They were both very tired by the time they reached Bethlehem. What a busy town it was! There seemed to be no room anywhere for the weary travellers from Bethlehem to stay the night. Joseph was anxious about Mary, and became worried when the last innkeeper they asked told him that he had not a single room left vacant in the inn.

Then, no doubt, he looked again at Mary and saw how tired she was, and he took pity on her. 'There is the stable where the animals are kept,' he suggested. 'You could shelter there for the night if you wish.'

Joseph was ready to take anything, for he could see that Mary was not fit to travel much further, and he readily agreed. At least the stable would provide shelter, and they could find a warm corner and lie down on some of the animals' straw.

Thankfully, they went into the stable, and during the night, with no one looking on except the animals, Mary's baby was born. She wrapped Him up in strips of cloth, called swaddling clothes. There was no cradle where she might lay her baby, so she put Him gently in a manger where hay was kept to feed the animals.

It was a strange arrival for the Son of God. But by allowing Jesus to be born in this humble way in the stable, God was showing that He was sympathetic to the poor and was the king of *all* people, not only of the rich and important. By living as the poorest, Jesus would show how He really understood them and took their part.

In the countryside, outside Bethlehem, a group of shepherds were looking after their sheep the night Jesus was born.

On this clear night, the Bethlehem shepherds wrapped their cloaks around them against the cold and talked among themselves. They gazed up at the night sky and saw many bright stars, but they were used to that.

Suddenly there seemed to be much more light than usual. The whole field was lit up with a brilliant radiance, and in the midst of it the shepherds saw the figure of an angel. They were terrified and covered their faces.

'Do not be afraid' said the angel, 'for I have brought you good news; news which will bring great joy to all the people. This very day in Bethlehem, the city of David, the Saviour of the world has been born. He is Christ the Lord.'

The shepherds were amazed; they could hardly take in such an important announcement.

The angel continued, 'As a sign to prove it to you, you will find the baby wrapped in swaddling clothes and lying in a manger.'

Hardly had the angel's words died away, than the whole sky surrounding the spot was filled with a multitude of angels. 'Glory to God in the highest,' they sang, 'and on earth peace to men with whom He is pleased.'

Then the angels went away, and the earth grew quiet and still.

The shepherds looked at one another in wonder. Was it true? Could they be dreaming? The Messiah, the Saviour of the world, here in Bethlehem? and in a *stable*? It did not seem possible.

Then one of the shepherds said, 'Come on, let's go and see this wonderful thing which the Lord has told us about through His angel.'

They hurried off, over the hills, and into Bethlehem.

But where should they look? Mangers were found only in stables, so they must look for a stable if they wanted to find the new-born king.

When at last they looked in at the stable belonging to the inn, they found the new baby, and they knelt down and worshipped Him.

Mary, His mother, and Joseph, her husband, were gazing fondly down at Him. The shepherds told them all that the angel had said, but Mary already knew something about her wonderful baby, for the angel Gabriel had told her whom He was to be. So she kept silent, but thought a great deal about the wonderful happening.

The shepherds, however, were greatly excited and returned to their sheep, singing praises to God. They had heard the angel and seen the baby; however much other people might find it hard to believe that God's Son had been born in a stable, they knew that it was true.

Forty days after Jesus was born, Mary and Joseph, according to the law, took Him to the temple in Jerusalem to be presented to God.

In Jerusalem at that time, there lived a good man whose name was Simeon. He was a God-fearing man, and it had been revealed to him that he would not die until he had seen the true Christ. It happened that he was in the temple when Mary and Joseph came in to present Jesus. As soon as Simeon saw Jesus he knew who He was and came forward at once.

Simeon took the baby in his arms and said, 'Lord, now let your servant go in peace, for I have seen the Saviour with my own eyes.'

Mary and Joseph were amazed at the things which Simeon said, for they were only slowly realizing the wonderful truth about their baby. Simeon blessed them too, and then he told Mary that Jesus would be the salvation of many in Israel, but that many people would speak against Him, and that she would suffer much sorrow.

The Visit of the Wise Men

Some time after the birth of Jesus, a group of rather important-looking men arrived in Jerusalem. They were men who studied the stars and their meanings, and were known as astrologers or 'wise men'.

They had come on a long journey from the east, from where, before they had begun their travels, they had seen a very bright new star in the sky. From their knowledge, they believed that this star meant the birth of the long-promised new King of the Jews. So, wanting to find out more, they had set off on their camels to follow the star.

When the star had led them as far as Jerusalem, the wise men began to ask people if this was where they would find the new king. 'Where is He who is born King of the Jews?' they asked. 'We have seen His star in the east, and have travelled here to worship Him.'

But no one in Jerusalem knew anything about a king being born there. So far as they knew, the only king in the area was Herod.

The news about the wise men's questionings reached the ears of King Herod, and he did not like the sound of it at all. He was a very jealous character, and he wanted no rivals to his throne or his power.

'A new king?' he thought, and became full of mistrust and suspicion. Not only was he troubled, but all the people of Jerusalem were troubled too, for when Herod was upset one never knew what he might do.

Herod summoned together all the chief priests and teachers of the law and asked them what they knew about it. 'Where will this Messiah, this King of the Jews, be born?' he asked in a pleasant, interested way.

They knew the answer to that one. It had been foretold by the prophet Micah hundreds of years earlier. He had written, 'And you, Bethlehem, in the land of Judah, are not the least of the cities of Judah, for from you there will come a ruler who will guide the people of Israel.' That could only mean the Messiah.

'Bethlehem,' thought Herod. 'Something must be done about this without delay.' So he summoned the wise men from the east to a secret conference. He found out from them at what time the star had appeared, and then he sent them off to Bethlehem to look for the new king whose birth seemed such a threat to him.

'Go and search very carefully for the young child,' he told them, 'and as

soon as you have found him, come back here and let me know; for I would like to go and worship him too.' Of course, Herod had no intention of going to worship a rival king. All he wanted was to find out where the child was so that he could have him removed as a rival to the throne and make sure that he, Herod, was the only king the Jews recognized.

The wise men left Jerusalem. They were pleased to see the star again and to follow it until it came to rest over a certain house in Bethlehem.

Joyfully the wise men went into the house where they saw the young child Jesus and His mother, and they knelt down and worshipped Him, happy that their long search was over.

Then, as it was the custom not to approach a monarch without bringing a gift, they presented their gifts to the new King of the Jews. They were royal gifts – gold, frankincense and myrrh – costly products of the countries from which the men had come.

While in Bethlehem the wise men had a dream, in which God warned them not to go back to King Herod, as he had requested; so they went back home another way, slipping quietly across the borders of Israel.

When the wise men did not return to Jerusalem, Herod realized that he had been tricked, and he flew into a furious rage. He gave orders that all baby boys in Bethlehem, who were two years old and under, were to be killed at once. That way, he thought, he would be sure to kill the new king among them.

Meanwhile, after the wise men had departed, Joseph also had a dream in which an angel appeared to him and said, 'Get up quickly, and take the young child, and Mary His mother, and escape into Egypt, for King Herod is looking for the child in order to kill Him.'

So that night, under cover of darkness, Joseph did as the angel had bidden him, and with Mary and Jesus he fled into Egypt, out of the range of Herod's power where they remained until the day that Herod died.

Then the angel appeared to Joseph in another dream and said, 'It is quite safe for you to take the child and His mother back to Israel now, for those who were searching for Him, to kill Him, are themselves now dead.'

So Joseph went to Galilee and there he, Mary and Jesus settled in Nazareth which lay in lower Galilee on the slopes of the Lebanon mountain range. Like Bethlehem it too was a quite unimportant town that was never to be forgotten because of its links with Jesus. And so it was in Nazareth that Jesus spent His boyhood.

Jesus as a Boy

As a boy, Jesus helped Mary in the everyday tasks of their humble home and also worked with Joseph in their carpenter's shop.

He was taught in the local synagogue by the rabbi or scribes, where He learned about the Jewish law, and every Sabbath He attended the synagogue for worship.

Every year Mary and Joseph used to journey to Jerusalem, like hundreds of other pilgrims, to celebrate the Passover.

When a Jewish boy was twelve years of age, he had to undergo preparation to become an adult in the religious community and to take his full part in the religious life of the village. From that time onward, he would no longer be looked upon as a child, but would be considered as a full member of the Jewish church. So, when Jesus was twelve, Mary and Joseph took Him to the festival at Jerusalem, so he too could take part in the ceremonies.

When the festival was over the people started to walk back home, but Jesus stayed behind in Jerusalem and did not set off back with His parents, although they did not realize this. No doubt they thought He was somewhere in the great company of people walking back — perhaps with relatives or friends, or with other boys of His own age, racing on ahead, or stopping to explore.

After they had been walking for a day, they made an evening halt, and it was then that Mary and Joseph found that Jesus was nowhere to be seen. Where could He be? Anxiously they asked around, but no one could recall seeing Him that day. Mary and Joseph became very worried and decided that the best thing to do was to retrace their steps to Jerusalem, in the hope that they would find him on the way. The next day, they set off back to the city, asking everyone they met whether they had seen Jesus, but no one could help them. At last they reached Jerusalem itself. After much worried searching, they finally found Jesus in the temple itself. He was sitting with a group of Jewish teachers, listening to them and asking them questions. The teachers were amazed at His understanding and at His intelligent questions and answers.

Mary and Joseph, too, were astonished. Mary said to Him, 'My son, why did you stay behind like this?

Why have you treated us so? We have been most worried trying to find you.'

Jesus was surprised that they did not know He would be in the temple. He asked, 'Did you not know that I had to be in My Father's house and about My Father's business?'

By His 'Father', He meant God; for even at that early age, He understood His special relationship with God the Father.

Mary and Joseph did not fully understand His answer, but Jesus then went back to Nazareth with them, and was obedient to them, thus showing His love and respect for them both.

Mary thought deeply about what had happened. She remembered the words of the angel Gabriel before Jesus was born, that her child was to be the Son of God; and also how the aged Simeon in the temple had called Jesus 'the Saviour'. She must have wondered what the future had in store.

The Baptism of Jesus

Some little time before Jesus was born, there lived an old priest of the temple named Zechariah. His wife was named Elizabeth and she was related to Mary, Jesus's mother. Both were good people, obeying God's laws, but they did not have any children and would have liked one very much. They had prayed for a child, but felt they were now too old.

Once a year Zechariah had to go to the temple at Jerusalem for two weeks to carry out his special duties as a priest.

As Zechariah was doing his turn of duty, he suddenly looked up and saw an angel at the right-hand side of the altar. He was alarmed and afraid at this strange sight.

'Don't be afraid, Zechariah,' said the angel, 'God has heard your prayers and you and Elizabeth will have a son. You will name him John and he will be a great man in God's

sight, filled with the Holy Spirit. He will prepare the way for the coming of the Lord.'

'But I am an old man,' said Zechariah, 'and my wife is old too. How can I know that what you say is so?'

'I am Gabriel,' the angel answered, 'I stand in God's presence, and it is He who has sent me to bring you this good news.'

In due time, Elizabeth had a baby boy, just as God had promised through the angel.

15

The time came for the baby to be given his name. Everyone thought he would be called Zechariah after his father, and they were very surprised when Elizabeth shook her head and said, 'No, he is going to be named John.'

As the boy John grew up he lived in the desert until the time came for him to begin his special work as a prophet among the people of Israel; the work for which God had sent him.

He was a strange, rugged-looking man, dressed in a garment made of cloth woven from camel's hair, with a leather belt round his waist. His food was strange too, for he ate locusts and wild honey.

Out of the desert came John, a stern, fiery prophet, calling upon the people to repent, to turn away from their sins and to begin a new way of life, because the Kingdom of God was near. News of him travelled fast, and crowds flocked to hear this strange new preacher.

'Prepare the way of the Lord,' cried John.

'Confess your sins, be truly sorry and come and be baptized,' called John, and hundreds of people came out to be baptized in the River Jordan. Being baptized meant being 'washed' and was a symbol of the cleaning up of the previous life. Because of this baptizing work, John came to be known as John the Baptist. Some people began to wonder if John was the expected Messiah. John told them, 'No, I am not

the Messiah, but there is One coming who is much greater than I am.'

One day John saw Jesus coming towards him. John pointed Him out to the people and said, 'Look, there He is! That is the One who will take away the sins of the world. It was He whom I was talking about when I said there was One coming who was much greater than me. I did not know who He was, but I came to baptize you with water, so that He might be known to the people of Israel.'

John was very surprised when Jesus came forward to the river to be baptized and felt that this was something which he could not do. Surely Jesus should be baptizing him instead, he thought. So he tried to prevent Jesus from being baptized, but Jesus told him it was God's will.

John agreed, and went into the river with Jesus to baptize Him, as was the custom in those days.

As soon as Jesus came up out of the river, it seemed that the heavens opened, and John saw the Holy Spirit, in the form of a dove, come down and alight on Jesus. At the same time a voice from heaven was heard saying, 'This is My beloved Son, with whom I am well pleased.'

These words showed that the baptism of Jesus did not mean that Jesus was a sinner who needed baptizing to wash away former sins like everyone else. God's words showed that Jesus was without sin but that He was now ready to identify Himself with all men and to take on the responsibility for their sin.

Temptation in the Wilderness

After Jesus's baptism by John, God led Him into the desert where He was tempted by the Devil. Jesus was in the desert for forty days and nights, preparing for, and thinking much about the work which He was to do. He knew that His power must serve men, who must only come to follow Him through their own free will.

In the first temptation from the Devil, the Devil asked Jesus, 'If you are really God's Son, command these stones to be turned into bread.'

Jesus replied, 'The scripture says, "Man shall not live by bread alone, but by every word which God speaks."'

Then the Devil tried a second temptation. He took Jesus to the highest point of the temple in Jerusalem and said, 'If you are God's Son, throw yourself down from the top here; you will be quite safe for the scriptures say that the angels will take care of you so that you won't be hurt on the stones.'

But Jesus firmly rejected this idea saying, 'The scripture also says. "Do not put God to the test."'

He did not want people to follow Him just because they were astounded at His miracles, but rather because they were truly attracted to His life and teaching.

Then the Devil had a third try. He took Jesus to the top of a very high mountain, from where he showed Him all the kingdoms of the world. 'All these', he said, 'I will give to you, if only you will worship me.'

Jesus gave him a plain, straightforward answer 'Go away. The scripture says, "Worship the Lord your God, and serve Him only."'

After this, the Devil gave up his hopeless task and left Jesus alone.

The Twelve Disciples

Now Jesus was ready to begin His work, and to do this He chose a band of twelve men to help Him.

One afternoon, John the Baptist was with two of his followers when he saw Jesus walking by. 'There He is!' John pointed out. 'That is the Lamb of God.'

One of the two men was named Andrew. When they heard what John said, they went after Jesus, and Jesus turned and saw them and they spent the rest of the day together.

Andrew was so impressed with Jesus that he immediately went and found his own brother, Simon. 'Simon, we have found the Messiah,' he said, and he took Simon to Jesus.

Jesus looked at Simon and knew what a great leader this man could be.

Both Andrew and Simon Peter were simple fishermen. They worked in their fishing business with two other brothers, James and John, who became disciples too.

These four attached themselves to Jesus and when they realized that He was the Messiah, they were ready to follow Him completely.

It happened that Jesus was walking along the shores of the Sea of Galilee one day when He again saw the fishermen at their work. Jesus saw two boats pulled up to the shore, one of which belonged to Simon Peter. He got into it and asked Simon to push it out a little way so that He could sit in it and teach the people on the shore more easily.

When He had finished speaking, He said to Simon Peter, 'Push your boat out further into the deep water and then let down your nets.'

'But master,' said Simon, 'we have been out all night and have caught nothing. Still, if You say so, we will obey.'

When the fishermen let down their nets they caught such a great number of fish that they had to signal to their partners in the other boat to come and help them. Both boats were soon full of fish.

On another day, when Jesus was in Galilee, He called a man named Philip to follow Him. Philip brought another future disciple, Nathanael, to Jesus.

When Jesus saw Nathanael coming towards Him, He said that here was an honest and true Israelite.

'How do you know me?' asked Nathanael, and Jesus replied that He had seen Nathanael under a fig-tree before Philip had even called him. Nathanael was quite astonished.

Another time Jesus saw a man who was a tax-collector sitting in his tax office, and said to him, 'Follow me,' and the man followed Him. He was Matthew.

The full list of the inner band of twelve is – Simon Peter, Andrew, James, John, Philip, Nathanael, Matthew, Thomas, another James, Thaddaeus, another Simon (the Zealot), and Judas Iscariot.

The Sermon on the Mount

The Sermon on the Mount is a collection of Jesus's teachings, which may not all have been given at one time. Most of Jesus's teaching was done in the open air, and we can imagine Him seated on a hillside with the crowds in their colourful robes gathered all about Him. They listened eagerly to what He was saying, for He spoke with great authority.

He showed that men ought not to live merely by a rigid set of rules, but rather by looking at life from God's point of view and by considering other people before themselves.

The Beatitudes

'Beatitude' means 'blessedness' or 'true happiness'.

Whereas people think that they must be rich or powerful in order to be happy, Jesus said that the truly happy person needs neither of these things.

He taught that the truly happy people are those who know they are spiritually poor and learn to rely on God; they are also those who are humble and who live as God wishes; those who are merciful and forgiving; those who are pure in heart, and those who are peacemakers.

The Work of His Disciples in the World

Jesus's followers are those who put 'seasoning' (salt) into life, and also those who light up the way for others. The things such people do and say help others to know something of what God is like. 'You are the salt of the earth', said Jesus, and also 'You are the light of the world.'

Teaching about the Law

Jesus said that He had not come to do away with the old law (the law which God had given Moses on Mount Sinai), but that He had come to fill it out, to extend it, and to show that it dealt not only with deeds, but with the thoughts which give rise to the deeds.

Not only is murder wrong, for example, but the kind of angry thought which could lead to murder is also wrong in itself.

Although the old law said 'an eye for an eye and a tooth for a tooth', Jesus said it is wrong to take vengeance on someone who has wronged you. That only makes a bad situation worse.

Jesus told people, 'Love your enemies and pray for those who terrorize you.' It used to be said that you should love your friends and hate your enemies. But there is nothing extraordinary in loving one's friends – anyone can do that – one must also deal kindly with those who are not one's friends.

Teaching about Prayer

Do not pray so that everyone will see you, but pray somewhere privately. Do not use long, meaningless words, but pray simply. Jesus then gave us a 'pattern prayer' like this, to help us pray.

'Our Father who art in heaven,
Hallowed be Thy Name,
Thy kingdom come,
Thy will be done, on earth as it is
in heaven.
Give us this day our daily bread;
And forgive us our debts, as we
also have forgiven our debtors;
And lead us not into temptation,
but deliver us from evil.

Teaching about Riches and Possessions

You can choose whether money and material things or God and spiritual things are your main aim in life, said Jesus.

Do not store up riches on earth, He advised, where moths and rust can get at them and thieves can break in and steal them. Put God first in your life, and He who knows all your needs will supply them. You will then have no need to worry.

You cannot put both God and material things first in your life. You must choose one; but where your heart is, that is where your riches really are.

Judging Others

Do not be critical of others when there is so much that can be criticized in your own life. Jesus said, humorously, that it is like a man who wanted to take a tiny speck out of his brother's eye, but did not notice that there was something the size of a great log in his own eye!

Having the Right Base for Your Life

'Anyone who hears My words and lives by them,' said Jesus, 'is like a man who builds his house on a rock – a firm foundation. The rains may pour down in torrents, and the winds may blow a terrible hurricane, and the floods may swell, but the house will not fall, beause it is standing firm on a rock.

'Anyone who hears My words and does not live by them is like a foolish man who builds his house on sand. Then, when the rains come in torrents, and the winds blow in a hurricane, and the floods swell, that house will crash down in ruins, because it was only built on sand which slips away.'

He meant that if you live by His standards, whatever storms and troubles come in life, they will be unable to defeat you.

Jesus Calms a Storm and Walks on the Water

At the end of one of the many days that Jesus spent teaching the people beside the Sea of Galilee, he said to the disciples, 'Let us cross to the other side of the lake.' So they left the crowd and climbed into a small boat and they began to row across.

The Sea of Galilee lies well below sea-level. All around there are hills, with deep ravines and gorges, and these act as funnels, drawing down the winds from the mountains. From time to time, these winds lash the waters into a great fury, making it dangerous for small boats.

Suddenly, as Jesus and the disciples were crossing, one of these great strong winds blew up, tossing the little boat about and putting them all in great danger of sinking or overturning.

The disciples were panic-stricken, even though some of them were experienced sailors. They turned to Jesus and found Him in the back of the boat — fast asleep, for He was tired after being with the crowds all day.

It seemed as though the little boat would be completely swamped by the raging waves, and the terrified disciples rushed to wake Jesus up. 'Master! Master! We are going to perish!' they cried. 'Don't you care?'

Calmly Jesus got up and said to the wind, 'Be quiet!', and to the waves He said, 'Peace, be still.'

And there was at once a great calm.

'Why were you so frightened?' asked Jesus of the disciples. 'Haven't you any faith?'

The disciples looked at one another in awe and wonder and said, 'What sort of man is this — that even the winds and the sea obey Him?'

Jesus Walks on the Water

Another time, by Galilee, Jesus asked the disciples to get into a boat and row across to Bethsaida at the other side of the lake. Meanwhile, He sent the crowd of people home and went up on the hillside by Himself to pray.

By evening time, the disciples in their little boat were far out on the lake, and were being tossed about somewhat, for it was a windy night and the sea was choppy.

In the early hours of the morning the disciples looked out and saw a figure walking towards them on the water. They were terrified and screamed with fear. 'It's a ghost!' they cried, their voices trembling.

Then the familiar and beloved voice of Jesus said, 'Do not be afraid. It is I.'

Now Peter, confident and enthusiastic as always, spoke up and said, 'Lord, if it is really You, tell me to come to You on the water.'

'Come,' said Jesus.

So Peter got out of the boat and began to walk on the water towards Jesus. But his faith did not last for long, and when he saw what a strong wind there was, he grew afraid – and as soon as he stopped trusting Jesus, he began to sink. 'Lord! Save me!' he cried out.

Jesus reached out and grabbed hold of his hand and said, 'What little faith you have! Why did you doubt?'

Then they both climbed into the boat, and the wind died down, the raging waves grew calm and the storm faded away.

The disciples turned to Jesus in awe saying, 'Truly, You are the Son of God.'

The Entry into Jerusalem

It was Passover time, a busy time in the city, when thousands of Jews were going up to the temple in Jerusalem to keep the festival, the great feast which commemorated the nation's deliverance from Egypt.

Jesus and His disciples were on their way to Jerusalem too, but the disciples could sense that this time their journey had a much more serious feel to it. Although they did not realize it at the time, this was the start of Jesus's last week of life on earth.

Jesus was very set and determined and walked on a little ahead of them. The people following were afraid, for they knew that the rulers wanted to seize Jesus, and by going into Jerusalem they felt that He was heading for certain capture.

Jesus took His twelve disciples aside and said to them, 'We are going to Jerusalem where the chief priests and rulers will condemn the Son of Man to death, and hand Him over to the Gentiles (non-Jews) who will mock, whip and crucify Him. But after three days He will rise again.'

He was talking about Himself and what was to happen, but the disciples did not understand.

As they drew near to the city, they came to Bethphage, which was close to Jerusalem, and near to the Mount of Olives. Here Jesus gave the disciples some special instructions. 'Go into the village over there,' He said, 'and you will find a colt (a young donkey) tied up, on which no one has ever ridden. Untie it and bring it to me. If anyone asks what you are doing, you are to say, "The Master needs it and will return it at once." Then the man will allow you to bring it to me.'

The disciples went and found the colt just as Jesus had said, and as they were untying it, the owners asked what they were doing. The disciples replied as Jesus had told them, and the owners said no more.

When the disciples brought the animal to Jesus, some of them threw their cloaks over it. Jesus mounted to ride the rest of the way into Jerusalem, and a great crowd went out to meet Him.

The Pharisees were most put out at this, and they said to one another in frustration, 'You see, we can do nothing; the whole world is following Him.'

The great crowd wanted to honour and praise Jesus as their king. Many knew that it was customary to put down a carpet for a king to walk on, and so they spread their brightly coloured cloaks in the path of Jesus to make a carpet for Him, as a gesture of respect. Other people climbed palm trees along the route, and cut down branches to wave or to spread along the road.

'Hosanna!' they cried, 'Praise to the Son of David! Blessed is He who comes in the name of the Lord! Praise God!'

There were crowds in front and crowds behind, so that the whole city was thrown into an uproar. Among the thousands who had gone up to Jerusalem for the Passover were some from far away places who had never heard anything about Jesus. So they asked, 'Who is He?'

'It is the prophet Jesus, from Nazareth in Galilee,' answered the people.

Some of the Pharisees in the crowd went up to Jesus and said, 'Command Your followers to be quiet.'

But Jesus answered, 'Even if they were quiet, the stones themselves would cry out instead.'

As He came closer to Jerusalem, Jesus wept and said to the city, 'If only you knew what is needed for peace! Yet you cannot see it. Your enemies will destroy you, because you have not recognized that God came to save you.'

That day was the first Palm Sunday.

Cleansing the Temple

The next day Jesus went into the temple. Now the temple was, in a special sense, the place of God's presence, although since the coming of Jesus, people have understood that God is everywhere and is not confined to a special place.

In the outer court of the temple, the Court of Gentiles, there were a number of money-changers working when Jesus went there.

Jews who came from other countries were not allowed to use their own foreign coins to pay the temple taxes, nor could they buy animals for sacrifice with anything but Jewish money. This meant that they had to go to the money-changers before they could take part in the festival.

Now the money-changers fixed a very dishonest rate of exchange and charged very high sums, even to the poorest people who could only afford the cheapest sacrifice, which was two pigeons.

Jesus was rightly very angry when He saw all the cheating and robbing that was going on within the temple area. He overturned the money-changers' tables and the stalls of those who were selling pigeons, and He drove all those who were doing such business out of the temple. 'My house is a house of prayer,' He cried, 'but you have made it a den of thieves!'

Then blind and crippled people came to Him to be healed and He healed them in the temple. The chief priests and lawyers were angry at the wonderful things He did, while they had turned a blind eye to the dishonesty of the money-changers.

The Last Supper

During the week which began with the first Palm Sunday came the Passover festival which was celebrated all over Israel.

Jesus and His disciples, who were now in Jerusalem, were also to celebrate the festival.

Jesus gave instructions to two of the disciples: 'Go into the city,' He said, 'and a man carrying a pitcher of water will meet you. Follow him into the house which he enters, and ask the householder where the room is where I am to eat the Passover with my disciples. He will show you an upper room and it is there that you

are to prepare the Passover. The rest of us will join you there.'

The two disciples went and found everything as Jesus had said.

In the evening of that day, Thursday, Jesus and His disciples assembled in the upper room. They did not know it then, but this was to be no ordinary Passover meal; Jesus was about to transform it into the Lord's Supper.

When the supper had been served, Jesus rose from the table, took off His outer garment, and tied a towel round His waist. Then He poured water into a basin and began to wash the disciples' feet.

The disciples had been arguing as to who was the greatest, and it seems that not one of them had wanted to do the menial act of feet-washing at the supper for fear of being thought less important than the others. So when Jesus saw that none of them offered to do this courteous act, He rose and willingly did it Himself for the whole company.

When He came to Simon Peter, that disciple protested, 'You shall never wash my feet, Lord. It is not right.'

'If I don't,' said Jesus, 'you have no part with me.'

Jesus meant that unless He washed Peter's sins from him, Peter had no link with Him.

Then Peter, perhaps beginning to understand, said, 'Lord, not only my feet, but also my hands and my head.'

When Jesus had washed all the disciples' feet, He returned to His place at the table.

As they were eating, Jesus said something startling. 'I tell you truly,' He said, 'that one of you will betray me.'

The disciples were puzzled and looked at one another in alarm. Then one of them asked Him whom He meant, and Jesus replied, 'It is the one to whom I give a piece of bread which I have dipped in the sauce of this dish.'

Then He took a piece of bread, dipped it, and gave it to Judas Iscariot. It was Jesus's last appeal to Judas, but Judas rejected it.

'Do quickly what you are about to do,' said Jesus to Judas, and again the disciples did not understand what Jesus meant, for they did not know that Judas was going to betray their master. Judas, after he had accepted the bread from Jesus, got up and went out into the night.

During the meal, Jesus did something wonderful. He took a piece of bread, said a prayer of thanks, broke the bread and gave it to His disciples saying, 'Take and eat; this is My body which is given for you.'

Then He took a cup of wine, gave thanks to God, and handed it to them saying, 'This is My blood which is poured out for many for the forgiveness of sins. Do this in memory of Me.'

Jesus tried to explain to the disciples why His death had to happen. 'I shall not be with you for very much longer,' He said, 'and you cannot come where I am going. Now I give you a new commandment, that you love one another. If you act in this way, then everyone will know that you are my disciples.'

'Why can't I follow You now?' asked Peter. 'I am ready to die for You.'

'Are you?' said Jesus sadly. 'I tell you that before the cock crows, you will have said three times that you did not know Me.'

'I'll never say that,' said Peter stoutly, 'even if I have to die with You.'

And the other disciples said the same, protesting their loyalty to Jesus.

Jesus told them much else about what was to happen. He would be returning to His Father and preparing the way for others to come to Him too. His return to God would bring them new power through the Holy Spirit; and the Holy Spirit would be with them all the time all over the world wherever they went.

Ever since that night Christians have held the service of the Lord's Supper or Holy Communion, in memory of that last meal which Jesus ate with his disciples.

The Garden of Gethsemane

Some time before the Last Supper, Judas had gone to the chief priests and had asked, 'How much will you give me if I betray Jesus to you?'

'Thirty silver coins,' they said.

From that time Judas kept on the lookout for an opportunity to betray his master. The chief priests and elders wanted Jesus arrested secretly, for they feared that if they took Him openly, there would be a riot among the people.

When the Passover meal, that Last Supper, ended, Jesus and the disciples sang a hymn and went to the Garden of Gethsemane, which was near the foot of the slopes of the Mount of Olives.

He asked Peter, James and John to keep watch, and went on a little further alone, to pray: 'Father, if it is possible, take this cup of suffering away from me; nevertheless, let not what I wish happen here, but what You wish.' And God sent Him the strength to go through with what was to happen.

Then He got up and went back to the three disciples, and found them asleep, for they were tired and worn out by grief and worry. Jesus said to Peter, 'Weren't you able to keep watch with me for even one hour? Watch and pray that you do not fall into temptation. The spirit is willing, but the flesh is weak.'

Jesus went back and prayed, and again when He returned, He found the disciples had fallen asleep. He went away and prayed a third time, and found the disciples sleeping once more when He came back to them. 'Are you still sleeping and resting?' He said. 'Look, the time has come for the Son of Man to be given over into the hands of wicked men. Rise up! Let us be going, for the man who is to betray Me is here.'

While Jesus was still speaking, a crowd of soldiers came into the garden, sent by the chief priests and elders. Among them was Judas. He had given them a signal, saying, 'The man I kiss is the one you are after. Go up and seize Him and lead Him away safely.'

Judas went up to Jesus and said, 'Hail, master!' and kissed Him.

'Do you betray the Son of Man with a kiss, Judas?' asked Jesus. Then He stepped forward and asked the soldiers, 'Whom do you seek?'

'Jesus of Nazareth,' they answered.

'I am He,' replied Jesus, and as He said this, they all moved back.

Then Simon Peter, who had a sword

with him, drew it and struck one of the high priest's servants. His name was Malchus, and the blow cut off his right ear.

'Enough of that!' said Jesus to Peter, and He touched Malchus's ear and healed it. 'Put your sword away. Do you think I will not drink the cup of suffering which My Father has given Me? Do not harm them.'

Jesus then turned to the soldiers and said, 'Did you have to come out to fetch Me with swords and clubs as though I were a robber? I was with you in the temple day after day, and yet you did not arrest Me there. This is the hour you act, when the power of darkness rules.'

And the disciples all deserted their master and ran away.

Then the soldiers and the temple guards took hold of Jesus, bound Him and took Him to the house of Annas who was the father-in-law of Caiaphas, the High Priest that year. He questioned Jesus about His disciples and His teaching and all the things He had done which had angered the high priests.

While this was going on, Simon Peter had been troubled in his conscience about forsaking Jesus, and he had secretly followed Him. He went into the courtyard of the High Priest's house, and the girl who kept the door said to him, 'Aren't you one of that man's disciples?'

'No,' said Peter, 'I am not. I don't even know Him.'

It was a cold night and so the servants and guards had made a charcoal fire and were standing by it and trying to get warm. Peter went over and stood with them.

Meanwhile Jesus was still being questioned, and Annas was trying to trap Him into saying that He had started a secret society. 'I have always spoken openly,' said Jesus to Annas. 'I taught in the synagogues and in the temple, where the Jews meet together. I said nothing secretly. Why don't you ask those who heard Me? They know what I said.'

At this, one of the guards standing by struck Jesus with his hand. 'How dare You speak so?' he said.

Jesus replied, 'If I have said anything wrong, tell Me, but if I have not, why do you hit Me?'

Then Annas sent Him, still bound, to Caiaphas.

Peter was still standing in the courtyard warming himself, and one of those present said, 'Aren't you one of that man's disciples? After all, your speech gives you away as a Galilean.'

'I am not,' said Peter again.

Then one of the servants of the High Priest spoke up. 'Did I not see you in the garden with Him?' he asked.

Again Peter answered, 'No', and immediately the sound of a cock crowing was heard. And Peter remembered how Jesus had said to him, 'Before the cock crows, you will deny Me three times.' Then he went away and wept bitterly.

The Trials and Crucifixion

Jesus was taken to the house of Caiaphas, the High Priest, where the lawyers and elders had gathered. They tried to produce false evidence against Jesus so that they could have Him put to death, but were unable to find any. Jesus kept silent until Caiaphas asked, 'Are You the Messiah, the Son of God?' Jesus replied, 'You have said so. I tell you all that you will see the Son of Man sitting at the right hand of God and coming on the clouds of heaven.'

'Blasphemy!' shrieked the High Priest in anger. 'You have just heard what He said. What do you think of that?'

'He is guilty and must die,' they replied full of rage and revenge.

Early the next morning Jesus was bound in chains and handed over to Pilate, the Roman governor. When Pilate saw Jesus before him, he asked, 'Are You the King of the Jews?'

'So you have said,' replied Jesus, but when the chief priests and elders made further accusations against Him, He did not answer.

'Do You hear all these things of which they are accusing You?' asked Pilate. But when Jesus still refused to answer, Pilate was amazed. 'I find no reason to condemn this man,' he said.

'His teaching is starting a riot,' the accusers urged. 'It began in Galilee and now He has come here.'

When Pilate heard that Jesus was a Galilean, and from the region ruled by Herod, Pilate sent Jesus to him. Herod had heard about Jesus's miracles, and hoped to see Him perform one. He asked Jesus many questions, but still Jesus refused to answer and Herod grew angry and returned Him to Pilate.

At every Passover, it was the custom for the governor to set free one prisoner – whichever one the crowds asked for. At that time a notorious bandit named Barabbas was being held.

When the crowd gathered, Pilate saw an opportunity to free Jesus. 'Which prisoner shall I set free?' he asked, 'Jesus or Barabbas?'

'Barabbas!' shouted the crowd, for the chief priests and elders had gone among the people persuading them to ask for Barabbas.

'What shall I do with Jesus then?' asked Pilate.

'Crucify Him,' they cried.

'But what crime has He committed?' asked Pilate, and for answer they shouted all the more, 'Crucify Him!'

So Barabbas was freed and Jesus was whipped and handed over to be crucified. Pilate's soldiers mocked Him, stripped off His clothes and put

a purple robe on Him. Then they made a crown of thorns and put it on His head, and placed a reed in His hand. 'Hail, King of the Jews!' they shouted.

Again Pilate tried to reason with the crowd, and again the crowd shouted, 'Crucify Him!

Then the crowd shouted to Pilate, 'If you set this man free, you're no friend of Caesar's.' Pilate feared the emperor, and so he handed Jesus over to the crowd to be crucified.

The Crucifixion

Crucifixion was a most horrible form of death. The victim was nailed to a cross and left hanging there to die in agony. He also had to carry his own cross to the site.

As Jesus was being led to the hill of Calvary, outside the city wall, He fainted under the weight of His cross, and a man named Simon from Cyrene was forced by the soldiers to carry it for Him.

Jesus was hung between two thieves. Above His head, Pilate had a notice placed reading, 'Jesus of Nazareth, King of the Jews.'

Jesus was on the cross for six hours, and during that time He spoke seven times.

First He prayed for the people and the soldiers saying, 'Father, forgive them for they do not know what they are doing.'

Then He spoke to one of the thieves who was repenting of his past, saying, 'Truly I say to you, today you will be with Me in paradise.'

Then He placed His mother Mary in the care of His disciple John: 'Woman, behold your son! John, behold your mother!'

Next, in great agony, He repeated some words from a psalm, 'My God, My God, why hast Thou forsaken Me?'

Then He said, 'I thirst', and a sponge soaked in cheap wine was passed up to Him, after which He said, 'It is finished.'

Finally, He prayed, 'Father, into Thy hands I commit My spirit,' and then He died.

For the last three hours that Jesus was on the cross, the sun ceased to shine, there was darkness over all the land and the curtain which hung in the temple was torn in two.

When Jesus had died, one of the soldiers plunged his spear into His side to make certain He was dead.

Among those who remained loyal to Jesus were two important men, who wished to see that He had a proper burial: Joseph of Arimathea, and Nicodemus. Joseph went to Pilate and asked if he could have Jesus's body. Pilate agreed, and with Nicodemus, Joseph took the body to the tomb which he had prepared for himself. Nicodemus brought costly spices with which to anoint the body, and they wrapped it in linen and laid it in the tomb. Then they placed a large heavy stone over the entrance.

Mary Magdalene, one of Jesus's followers, and another woman called Mary were watching and they saw where the body of Jesus was lain and went to tell the disciples.

So ended the first Good Friday.

The First Easter Day

Very early in the morning, two days after Jesus's crucifixion, Mary Magdalene and some other women went to His tomb, taking some sweet-smelling spices for His body. As they drew near, they saw to their surprise that the stone which blocked the entrance had been moved.

The women crept up to the tomb and looked inside – the body of Jesus had gone! Two angels stood where His body had lain. 'Don't be afraid,' said the angels. 'Why are you looking for the living among the dead? Jesus is not here. He has risen. He told you that He would be crucified but would rise again on the third day. Go and tell His disciples, and Peter, that He is going before you into Galilee, and there you will see Him.'

The women ran back to Jerusalem to tell the disciples, but the disciples didn't believe them. However, after a while Peter and John decided to go and see for themselves.

John arrived first and stooped down to look inside. Certainly Jesus's body had gone, but the grave-clothes were still there. No one would have removed the grave-clothes before taking Jesus's body away. It was as though the body had miraculously passed through them.

Then Peter went into the tomb, followed by John – and they saw and believed, but did not understand what had happened. Feeling very puzzled, they returned home.

Mary Magdalene went back to the tomb, and stood outside it weeping. She too looked inside; two angels sat where the body of Jesus had been. They asked her, 'Why are you weeping?'

Mary replied, 'Because they have taken away my Lord, and I do not know where they have put Him.'

As she said this, she turned and saw someone standing there, but she could not see clearly who it was. 'Woman, why are you weeping? Who is it that you are looking for?' the figure asked.

Mary said, 'Sir, if you have taken Him, tell me where you have laid Him, and I will take Him away.'

Then He said, 'Mary!', and Mary knew it was Jesus!

'Teacher!' she said to Him.

'Don't touch Me,' said Jesus, 'for I have not yet gone back to My Father; but go and tell My brothers that I am returning to My Father and their Father, to My God and their God.'

Joyfully Mary went to the disciples to tell them the exciting news. She had seen Jesus! And she told them all that He had said.

The Ascension and First Whitsunday

For forty days after Jesus had risen from the dead on the first Easter Sunday He was seen by many of His friends at various times. There could be no doubt that He was alive again and had risen from the dead, just as He had said He would.

When He came in the midst of them like that He always knew what had been happening just beforehand. Gradually they began to realize that whether they could see Him or not, whether they could hear Him or not, He was always with them and this gave them great comfort.

During this time the disciples listened hard to what He told them, learning no doubt that they would be expected to carry on His work. For He knew that the time was coming when He would have to leave them in bodily form, and they would no longer see and hear Him on earth.

He charged the disciples: 'Go into all the world and make people My disciples, baptizing them in the name of the Father, and of the Son, and of the Holy Spirit, and teaching them to obey My commands. And I will be with you always, even until the end of the world.'

Now on the fortieth day after the resurrection, He had led them out as far as Bethany and on to a hill. He had given them special orders that they were not to leave Jerusalem until they received the gift of the Holy Spirit, which would strengthen them for the task of winning the world for God – a seemingly impossible job for such a small band of men. However, Jesus knew that with God all things are possible, and He said, 'When the Holy Spirit comes to you, you will be filled with power and will be My witnesses in Jerusalem, in all Judea and Samaria, and to the ends of the earth.'

After He had said this, He blessed them, and then a cloud covered Him and took Him up out of their sight.

As the disciples stood gazing at the sky, two angels appeared beside them and said, 'You men of Galilee, why are you standing gazing up into heaven? Jesus, who was taken from you into heaven, will come back in the same way that you have seen Him depart from you into heaven.'

Although the disciples would see Jesus no more, they felt happy and returned to Jerusalem with great joy. They were happy because He had blessed them, and full of joy that He would always be with them.

Now they could look forward to the coming of God's Holy Spirit, which would give them power and strength for the great work which was ahead.

The First Whitsunday

After Jesus's ascension into heaven, the disciples went back to Jerusalem. They were still afraid of the Jewish authorities who had killed Jesus, so they stayed indoors where they felt safer. Each day after the ascension they wondered if the gift of the Holy Spirit would come that day and they watched and waited.

A week went by, then eight days, nine days, and, at last, on the tenth day something strange and wonderful happened.

Now the tenth day happened to be the feast of Pentecost. Pentecost means 'fifty', and this feast always came fifty days after the Passover. Pentecost marked the end of the barley harvest, when the Jews presented freshly baked loaves of new, fine, leavened flour in the temple. It was a day of rejoicing and gratitude for the gifts of the earth – rather like a harvest festival.

Jesus's band of inner disciples now numbered twelve again, for a new man named Matthias had been chosen to replace Judas Iscariot, who had killed himself after his evil deed of betrayal on that night in the Garden of Gethsemane.

This band of twelve are known as the twelve apostles – the word 'apostle' means 'one who is sent' (to preach and teach). The world 'disciple' means 'learner' – all those who followed Jesus, believed in Him and wanted to obey His teachings were considered to be disciples, including the apostles.

On this day of Pentecost, the apostles and probably some other disciples were all gathered together in one place.

Suddenly there was a loud noise, like a rushing mighty wind, and it filled the whole house where they were sitting. They looked at one another in astonishment and saw a glowing light split up into what looked like flames of fires hovering above each of their heads. This was the outward sign that the promised gift of God's Holy Spirit had now come to them.

The mighty wind was a symbol of the power and energy of the Holy Spirit, and the flames of fire were a symbol of the fiery zeal with which the disciples would now be able to proclaim the Gospel.

The effect on them was tremendous. No longer were they weak, cowering, frightened people; instead they felt strong and brave and were filled with a great strength.

The disciples felt filled with such courage and strength that they immediately left the house and went among the crowds of people outside. These included not only those who lived in Jerusalem, but also countless visitors who had come to Jerusalem for the feast of Pentecost. There were Parthians, Medes and Elamites, representing countries from beyond the influence of the Roman Empire; there were people from Mesopotamia, from Judea, from Cappadocia, Asia Minor, Pamphylia, Egypt and Libya, Crete and Arabia.